I0755911

For Pete's Sake

A Celebration of Caucasian Conversation

Erin Tyler

For Pete's Sake

For permissions or licensing inquiries, contact:
Switch Kick Books
SwitchKickBooks@gmail.com

ISBN: 979-8-89814-531-6
Printed in USA
First Edition

Written, designed, illustrated by Erin Tyler.

For Carol.

My favorite funny white lady.

Books
are
magic

Introduction

LET'S FACE IT—every culture has its quirks, but there's something particularly charming (and hilarious) about the things white people say. This book is a loving, tongue-in-cheek celebration of the weird, wonderful, and wildly specific phrases that have somehow become part of the great suburban soundtrack of life.

If you've ever heard someone say "Yeah? You and what army, pal?" when feeling even mildly threatened, or mutter "Jeez Louise" under their breath like it's a legally binding oath, congratulations—you've been in the presence of peak Caucasian phraseology. These sayings are part of a deeply committed cultural tradition—somewhere between small talk and performance art.

This isn't about mockery—it's about marveling. Marveling at how entire conversations can be built out of mindless weather commentary, mild exclamations, and passive-aggressive phrases passed down through generations of dads who barbecue in socks and sandals and moms whose haircuts border on "Karens."

So unzip your cargo pants into shorts, fill up your Stanley, and prepare to dive into a delightful compendium of expressions that are equal parts confusing, comforting, and absurd.

Welcome to *For Pete's Sake: A Celebration of Caucasian Conversation*. Buckle up—it's gonna be a hoot and a holler![1]

---

1 A *really* good time.

FOLKSY OLD-FARTISM

When you mess with the bull, you get the horns!

A DIRE WARNING TO ANY POTENTIAL OPPONENT.

Yeah? You and what army, tough guy?

WHEN SOMEONE NEEDS TO BE "KNOCKED DOWN A PEG."

FOLKSY OLD-FARTISM

Hot diggity dog!

WHEN EXCITED ABOUT JUST ABOUT ANYTHING. OFTEN ACCOMPANIED BY A CLAP, OR KNEE SLAP.

I'm not gonna take any guff from you.

"I'M NOT PUTTING UP WITH YOUR CRAP." SAID TO A SPIRITED YOUNG "WHIPPERSNAPPER."

MILLENNIAL MOM

Mercury must be in retrograde.

A VERSATILE PHRASE MEANT TO EXPRESS MILD DISTRESS, OR FRUSTRATION WITH TECHNOLOGY.

I set an intention for that.

USED WHEN THEY WANT TO "MANIFEST" SOMETHING.

That doesn't serve me anymore.

"F*CK THAT SH*T."

Dave
Matthew
Band

WHITE DAD

Get a load of this guy.

A CHEEKY EXPRESSION MEANING "CHECK THIS GUY OUT." PAIRED WITH A THUMB IN THE DIRECTION OF THE "GUY."

That's not going anywhere.

AFTER TYING SOMETHING DOWN WITH ROPES, CORDS OR BUNGEES.

FOLKSY OLD-FARTISM

Golly gee willikers!

MEANING: "WOW!"

BOOMER HALL-OF-FAMER

I know I'm gonna butcher this.

BEFORE PRONOUNCING A FOREIGN NAME.

FOLKSY OLD-FARTISM

I like the cut of his jib.

"I LIKE THAT GUY."

Don't put the coffee on. We're not staying.

AFTER PULLING INTO A STRANGER'S DRIVEWAY TO TURN AROUND.

WHITE DAD

Looks like we got here just in time.

WHEN A CROWD OF PEOPLE SHOW UP AT A RESTAURANT AT WHICH YOU'VE ALREADY BEEN SEATED.

Let's blow this Popsicle stand.

WHEN IT'S TIME TO LEAVE SAID RESTAURANT. DOESN'T HAVE TO BE A POPSICLE STAND.

BOOMER HALL-OF-FAMER

I'm gettin' a contact high.

WHEN THEY SMELL MARIJUANA BEING SMOKED AT A CONCERT.

Wacky Tobacky.

WHAT THEY CALL THE MARIJUANA BEING SMOKED AT THE CONCERT.

MILLENNIAL MOM

Are your beans fair-trade?

Do you have any stevia?

Iced White Chocolate Mocha, extra whip, extra caramel drizzle.

AT STARBUCKS, OR ANY COMPARABLY FANCY COFFEE SHOP.

fancy
pants
COFFEE

FOLKSY OLD-FARTISM

Kick rocks!

"GET LOST."

You don't know shit from Shinola.

NO ONE KNOWS WHAT SHINOLA IS.

WHITE DAD

Yel-*low*!

WHILE ANSWERING A PHONE CALL.

You are!

COMMON REPLY TO THE QUESTION "IS ANYONE SITTING HERE?"

What's the good word?

"HOW ARE YOU DOING?"

FOLKSY OLD-FARTISM

That dog won’t hunt.

WHEN THE PLAN IS NOT GOING TO WORK.

Hasn't got a pot to piss in.

ABOUT SOMEONE WHO IS BROKE.

That's rich coming from you.

"YOU'VE GOT SOME NERVE!"

MILLENNIAL DAD

What's the IBU of this IPA?

"HOW BITTER IS THIS CRAFT BEER?"

Whole Foods? More like *Whole Paycheck*.

USUALLY FOLLOWED BY A CHUCKLE.

FARMERS
MARKET

ALL-PURPOSE WHITE SPEAK

Per my last email...

A PASSIVE-AGGRESSIVE REMINDER THAT YOU FORGOT SOMETHING.

Living the dream!

WHEN ASKED HOW THEY ARE DOING.

IF ASKED ON A WEDNESDAY, THEY WILL FORGO THIS RESPONSE FOR SOMETHING HUMP-DAY RELATED. WHITE PEOPLE LOVE HUMP-DAY.

Working hard, or hardly working?

A GREETING COMMONLY USED WHILE VISITING A CO-WORKER'S DESK.

Assistant
to the
Regional
Manager

FOLKSY OLD-FARTISM

BOOMER HALL-OF-FAMER

Here comes trouble!

Look what the cat dragged in!

BOTH UTTERED WHEN A GOOD BUDDY ARRIVES.

ALL-PURPOSE WHITE SPEAK

Tee Mar-two-nis.

INSTEAD OF TWO MARTINIS.

That'll put hair on your chest!

AFTER SAMPLING A STRONG DRINK.

LIVE
LAUGH
LOVE

ALL-PURPOSE WHITE SPEAK

Let me just scooch in.

See ya later, alligator.

COMMONLY FOLLOWED BY "AFTER A WHILE, CROCODILE."

ALL-PURPOSE WHITE SPEAK

Exsqueeze me.

"EXCUSE ME."

There's no excuse for ya!

A REPLY TO "EXCUSE ME."

I'll be there in a jiffy.

THIS MEANS–ROUGHLY–"AS SOON AS POSSIBLE."

ALL-PURPOSE WHITE SPEAK

You're barking up the wrong tree, pal.

WHEN SOMEONE DOESN'T KNOW WHO THEY'RE "MESSING WITH."

Alright, that *tears* it!

WHEN THEY'VE "HAD IT UP TO HERE" WITH SOMEONE'S BEHAVIOR.

FOLKSY OLD-FARTISM

BOOMER HALL-OF-FAMER

I'll be sure to stay off the road!

SAID TO A TEENAGER WHO HAS JUST GOTTEN THEIR DRIVER'S LICENSE.

Put that in your pipe and smoke it!

SO THERE!

MILLENNIAL MOM

Is it wine-o'clock yet?

ONE CAN ASK IF IT IS "BEER-O'CLOCK" AS WELL, DEPENDING ON BEVERAGE PREFERENCES.

ALL-PURPOSE WHITE SPEAK

It's 5-o'clock somewhere!

COMMONLY SAID AROUND 4PM. EARLIER IF IT HAS BEEN A ROUGH DAY.

I hope
you brought
wine

Smooth move, Ex Lax.

"WAY TO GO, DUMB*SS."

Ope! They found ya!

SAID WHEN POLICE CAR SIRENS ARE HEARD IN THE VICINITY.

FOLKSY OLD-FARTISM

BOOMER HALL-OF-FAMER

Thanks, Captain Obvious.

"THANKS, BUT NO THANKS."

Don't you look spiffy!

A HIGH CAUCASIAN COMPLIMENT.

Renaissance

FOLKSY OLD-FARTISM

Jiminy Crickets!

ONE CAN ALSO SAY "JIMINY CHRISTMAS."

Holy smokes!

Heavens to Betsy!

EXCLAMATIONS OF EXCITEMENT.

I don't give a rat's ass!

SAID WHEN "MIFFED", OR TOTALLY OVER SOMEONE'S 'TUDE.

LET'S
COOK

ALL-PURPOSE WHITE SPEAK

It was *terrible*.

WHEN THE WAITRESS CLEARS AN EMPTY PLATE, AND ASKS HOW THE MEAL WAS.

That's got a little kick to it.

AFTER EATING MILDLY SPICY FOOD.

What's the damage?

WHEN THE CHECK ARRIVES TO THE TABLE AT A RESTAURANT.

Family
fecipe
Real
Mayonnaise
SMOOTH AND CREAMY
NET WT. 12 OZ [.35L]

PURE MIDWEST

Oofta!

A SPECIAL–MINNESOTA-SPECIFIC–REPLY MEANING "GOODNESS," OR "OH MY." SOMETIMES SPELLED "UFFDA."

Oh, fer cute!

EQUALLY MINNESOTAN PHRASE, MEANING "HOW CUTE!"

FOLKSY OLD-FARTISM

Hay is for horses.

A RESPONSE TO "HEY!"

Well I'll be a monkey's uncle!

"WELL, HOW ABOUT THAT." ONE OF THE MORE BIZARRE IDIOMS WHITE PEOPLE LIKE TO USE.

Can it, buddy!

"SHUT UP."

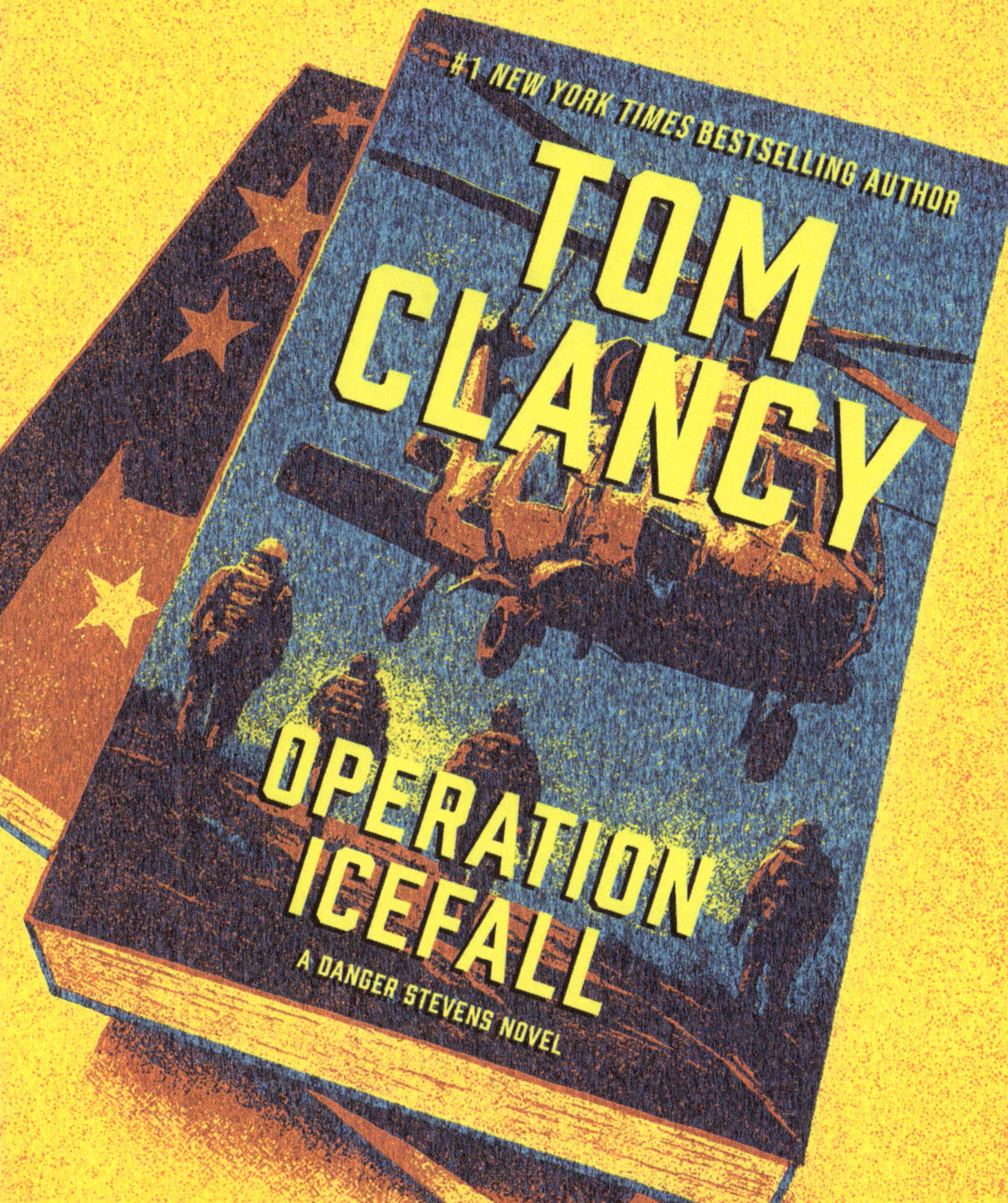
#1 NEW YORK TIMES BESTSELLING AUTHOR
TOM CLANCY
OPERATION ICEFALL
A DANGER STEVENS NOVEL

FOLKSY OLD-FARTISM

Dag nabbit!

A WAY OF SWEARING WITHOUT ACTUALLY SWEARING. CAN BE SWAPPED OUT WITH ANY OF THE FOLLOWING: "DOGGONE IT", "CONSARN IT", "FIDDLESTICKS", "SON OF A BISCUIT", AND/OR "CRIMINY!"

What am I? Chopped liver?

SAID WHEN IN NEED OF ATTENTION OR AFFECTION.

ASK ME
ABOUT
CROSSFIT

FOLKSY OLD-FARTISM

BOOMER HALL-OF-FAMER

Hold yer horses.

"WAIT A MINUTE!"

Pump the brakes, pal.

"I SAID WAIT A MINUTE, MISTER!"

Cool your jets, buddy!

"I'M AT MY *WIT'S END* WITH YOU!"

EMOTIONAL
SUPPORT PONY

ALL-PURPOSE WHITE SPEAK | PURE MIDWEST

Okey dokey, artichokey.

"OKAY."

You betcha.

Oh yah.

Yeppers.

"YES."

FOLKSY OLD-FARTISM | BOOMER HALL-OF-FAMER

Jesus, Mary and Joseph!

Jeez Louise.

EXCLAMATIONS OF DISTRESS. NO ONE KNOWS WHO LOUISE IS.

You're cruisin' for a bruisin', buster.

A VERSATILE WARNING THAT CAN BE SAID TO ALL "BUSTERS" AND ALSO ALL "NON-BUSTERS."

ALL-PURPOSE WHITE SPEAK

Fuhgeddaboudit.

PHRASE COMMONLY USED IN AN ITALIAN RESTAURANT. NO ONE KNOWS WHAT IT MEANS. MUST BE PRONOUNCED WITH A JERSEY ACCENT. AT IT'S BEST WHEN PERFORMED WITH A GLASS OF RED WINE IN HAND.

Don’t make me turn this car around.

THE CAR IS ALMOST NEVER TURNED AROUND.

Don't talk to me till I've had my coffee.

COMMON MORNING PHRASE, ALONG WITH "TIME TO MAKE THE DONUTS."

Sustainably
Sourced
COFFEE

ALL-PURPOSE WHITE SPEAK

Okay, just one bite.

SAID BEFORE EATING THE TOTALITY OF A DESSERT.

Well there's my cardio for the day!

AFTER WALKING UP A FLIGHT OF STAIRS.

Let's
Brunch
MENU
FRENCH TOAST

FOLKSY OLD-FARTISM | BOOMER HALL-OF-FAMER

We sure needed it.

A COMMENT MADE AFTER A HEAVY RAINFALL.

It's not the heat that gets ya. It's the humidity.

CLASSIC HOT TAKE ON FLORIDA WEATHER. LITERALLY A HOT TAKE.

Afterword

WELL I'LL BE DARNED, YOU MADE IT TO THE END!

IF YOU'VE READ THIS FAR, *bless your heart.* Hopefully you've either recognized half these phrases from your own vocabulary, chuckled at the ones your parents or grandparents used to say, or furiously highlighted them for future anthropological research. Either way, thanks for coming along on this weird little linguistic road trip.

I wrote *For Pete's Sake*[2] because, honestly, I couldn't help but marvel at the way hearing someone say, "Don't make me turn this car around" can instantly summon the ghost of every sweaty summer road trip past in the family station wagon. How a simple "Look what the cat dragged in," takes me straight to green plastic bowls of noodle salads at 4th of July get togethers. Or how much "Heavens to Betsy" reminds me of the people who made me who I am. Sure, some of these expressions might be outdated. Some are confusing. Some are so deeply suburban they practically smell like freshly mowed lawn and boxed wine. But all of them carry a certain charm—one that's equal parts humor and *why the hell do we say that*?

It's about looking around—at ourselves, our families, our neighbors—and appreciating the strange beauty of how we talk to each other. How we connect. How we say "See ya later, alligator," eliciting an instinctual

"After a while, crocodile," and then bask in the warmth of neighborly affection.

So whether you're a lifelong practitioner of Caucasian Phraseology or just dipping your toes into the Aqua Velva-scented waters, I hope this book made you laugh, and provided a little insight into what makes this specific brand of speak so wonderfully uncool.

And remember:

If someone gives you trouble, tell 'em they're "Cruisin' for a bruisin'."

If all else fails, just scooch on out and say, "Let's blow this popsicle stand."

And most importantly, don't take any guff from a whippersnapper until you've had your coffee.

—Erin Tyler

PFLUGERVILLE, TEXAS
JUNE, 2025

---

2 **No one knows who "Pete" is.**

www.ingramcontent.com/pod-product-compliance
Lightning Source LLC
LaVergne TN
LVHW071451110826
845155LV00045B/17

* 9 7 9 8 8 9 8 1 4 5 3 1 6 *